POINTS OF VIEW

I0811209

# Are KIDS TOO BUSY?

By Katie Kawa

KidHaven PUBLISHING

Published in 2025 by
**KidHaven Publishing, an Imprint of Greenhaven Publishing, LLC**
2544 Clinton St.
Buffalo, NY 14224



Designer: Deanna Paternostro
Editor: Katie Kawa

Photo credits: Cover, p. 11 (top) Prostock-studio/Shutterstock.com; p. 5 (top) SrideeStudio/Shutterstock.com; pp. 5 (bottom), 7 (top left), 9, 17 Monkey Business Images/Shutterstock.com; pp. 7 (top right), 21 (inset left) Dmytro Zinkevych/Shutterstock.com; p. 7 (bottom left) VGstockstudio/Shutterstock.com; p. 7 (bottom right) BongkarnGraphic/Shutterstock.com; p. 11 (bottom) PeopleImages.com - Yuri A/Shutterstock.com; p. 13 karelnoppe/Shutterstock.com; p. 15 SynthEx/Shutterstock.com; p. 19 SpeedKingz/Shutterstock.com; p. 21 (notepad) ESB Professional/Shutterstock.com; p. 21 (markers) Kucher Serhii/Shutterstock.com; p. 21 (photo frame) FARBAI/iStock/Thinkstock; p. 21 (inset right) kornnphoto/Shutterstock.com.

**Cataloging-in-Publication Data**

Names: Kawa, Katie.
Title: Are kids too busy? / Katie Kawa.
Description: Buffalo, NY : KidHaven Publishing, 2025. | Series: Points of view | Includes glossary and index.
Identifiers: ISBN 9781534547704 (pbk.) | ISBN 9781534547711 (library bound) | ISBN 9781534547728 (ebook)
Subjects: LCSH: Time management–Juvenile literature. | Student activities–Juvenile literature. | After-school programs–Juvenile literature. | Anxiety in children–Juvenile literature.
Classification: LCC BF637.T5 K38 2025 | DDC 155.4'19–dc23

Printed in the United States of America



CPSIA compliance information: Batch #CSKH25: For further information contact Greenhaven Publishing LLC at 1-844-317-7404.

Please visit our website, www.greenhavenpublishing.com. For a free color catalog of all our high-quality books, call toll free 1-844-317-7404 or fax 1-844-317-7405.

# CONTENTS

# Finding Your VOICE

What do you do after school? Some kids go to soccer practice, while others rush to dance class. Some meet with a **tutor** to get help with math or learn another language. There are also kids who go straight home after school, do their homework, and spend the rest of their night on their phone, playing video games, or watching TV.

Some people think it's important for kids to stay busy. However, many people have argued that kids today—especially in the United States—are too busy. It's important to understand both sides of this **debate** before you choose which side you agree with.

Adults are often worried about kids being too bored and about them being too busy, but what do kids think? This is a debate about kids, so it's important for kids to develop, or form, their own opinion and find their own voice in the debate.

## Know the Facts!

The U.S. government reported that more kids between the ages of 6 and 17 took part in after-school activities in 2020 than in 1998. For example, in 1998, around 30 percent of girls in this age group played a sport after school. By 2020, around 35 percent of girls played an after-school sport.

# What Do KIDS DO?

Many different activities can keep kids busy. Some are things kids have to do, such as homework. Parents or guardians might also add extra learning activities for kids after school. This can include meetings with a tutor to improve their grades or private music or language lessons.

Clubs also keep kids busy. Members of clubs might meet to build robots, put on plays, or create a school newspaper. Many kids are part of sports teams too. In fact, more than half of all kids in the United States played a sport in 2020.

**Know the Facts!**

According to the U.S. government, 27 percent of boys and 37 percent of girls ages 6 to 17 took after-school lessons of some kind in 2020. These included lessons in dance, music, and languages.

Some kids take part in one activity after school, while others do many different things. Some kids also **volunteer** after school or on weekends. They do things like cleaning up neighborhoods, planting community gardens, and reading to dogs and cats at animal **shelters**.

# No Time to REST

With so many different activities to choose from, many people believe it's easy to see how kids can become overscheduled. This means having too many things planned and not enough free time. Between homework, sports practices and games, lessons, club meetings, and volunteer work, some people argue that there isn't enough time for kids to rest.

Rest is important for kids' **mental** health. Many kids deal with mental health problems, such as **anxiety**. People have argued that being overscheduled can cause anxiety in kids. They believe if kids had more free time, they might feel less **stressed**.

## Know the Facts!

By 2020, 5.6 million kids in the United States were diagnosed with, or formally said to have, problems with anxiety.

Many kids have to do their homework after they come home from after-school activities. This can keep them from getting enough sleep. More than half of all students in middle school don't get the amount of sleep doctors say they need.

# ON THE RISE

Some people believe the rise in anxiety among kids is a sign that they're too busy. However, other people argue that many activities are actually helpful for kids' mental health. Some activities, such as playing sports, have been shown to help kids develop a strong sense of self-esteem, which means a positive way of seeing themselves.

While anxiety is a big problem among kids, so is loneliness. Feelings of loneliness among young people are on the rise. People have argued that one way to fight this is to keep kids busy with activities where they can make friends.

**Know the Facts!**

Studies have shown that adults who report feeling very lonely often report that they also felt lonely as kids. Loneliness can play a part in health problems, so **experts** agree that making connections with others is important.

During the **COVID-19 pandemic**, most after-school activities stopped, and kids weren't as busy as they were before. More than half of all parents who took part in a study during this time were worried about their kids not having after-school activities and not making connections with friends.

# When Do They PLAY?

When kids are busy with many different activities, they often make friends. However, they're often connecting with those friends in a structured way, which means with rules to follow, set activities to do, and often an adult constantly watching them. They don't have the same kind of freedom that playing with their friends in a less structured way would give them.

People who think kids are too busy often state that kids don't have enough time to play—both with friends and by themselves. This can be seen as a problem because playtime helps with creativity, imagination, and learning.

## Know the Facts!

In a 2023 report, experts stated that one of the reasons for the rise in anxiety among kids is the lack of time to independently play because they're too busy. These experts said independent play can help kids feel more confident, or sure of themselves, and less afraid.

Having time to play is important for kids. Some people are worried that kids are missing out on learning important life skills and making fun memories because they're too busy to play.

# Free Time Equals SCREEN TIME

Most people agree that kids need time to play. However, some people argue that kids don't use the free time they have now to play. Instead, they spend it looking at screens.

According to the U.S. government, kids between the ages of 8 and 10 spend around 6 hours a day looking at screens for fun. This has caused some people to think that kids aren't busy enough. They believe kids need to spend more time taking part in activities so they have less time to spend using **social media** or watching TV.

### Know the Facts!

Spending too much time looking at screens, especially using social media, has been connected to anxiety and other mental health problems in kids.

Screen time can include time spent using social media, watching videos or TV shows, and playing video games. Some people believe keeping kids busy with different activities is a good way to fight the harmful effects of too much screen time, such as sleep problems and lower self-esteem.

# What's the COST?

When kids are busy, parents, guardians, and other family members are busy too. Adult family members often need to drive busy kids to practices, games, lessons, and other activities. Then, they need to pick them up when it's done or stay to cheer them on. This can make it harder for the entire family to spend time together during the week.

Being busy costs time—and it also costs money. Adults often have to pay for things such as dance lessons or trips for travel sports teams. This can cause extra stress for some families.

**Know the Facts!**

In 2023, the average amount of money parents and guardians spent on their kids' after-school activities was $731.

People who believe kids are too busy often argue that kids' activities are costing families too much time and money. For example, many families think it's important to have dinner together, but kids' activities can sometimes make that impossible.

# Safe and SUCCESSFUL

Most people agree that quality family time is a good thing for kids—and all family members—to have. However, having everyone home at the same time isn't the **reality** for a lot of families—even those with kids who aren't very busy. Adults' work hours sometimes mean that kids come home to an empty house after school.

This is one reason why some people argue that keeping kids busy is good for them. It gives them something to do after school, especially if their parents or guardians are still working. This can help keep them safe.

**Know the Facts!**

A report from 2020 showed that 20 percent of young people in the United States came home to an empty house after school.

Staying busy can help kids feel safe and successful. It's been shown that taking part in after-school activities can help kids get into college after finishing high school. Some students earn scholarships, or money for college, if they're very successful in an activity such as playing a sport or an instrument.

# Your Opinion MATTERS!

Now that you've learned the facts and studied the arguments used by people on both sides of this debate, you can share your own informed, or educated, opinion. Do you think kids are too busy?

This debate has been going on for a long time, and people have many different points of view about how busy kids are in general. However, when it comes to how busy you are, your point of view matters most! If you feel like you're too busy and it's causing you stress or anxiety, talk to a trusted adult.

### Know the Facts!

Some signs that you might be too busy include feelings of anxiety, stomachaches, headaches, and feeling tired. Being too busy can also cause poor grades because you don't have enough time to study for tests or do homework.

# Are kids too busy?

## YES

- Anxiety is on the rise in kids, and being overscheduled is a cause of anxiety.
- Kids don't have time to play, and playtime is important for learning, creativity, and mental health.
- Families don't spend as much quality time together because they have to take kids to and from activities.
- Parents and guardians spend a lot of money on kids' activities.

## NO

- Loneliness is on the rise in kids, and taking part in a lot of activities can help kids make friends.
- Kids spend the free time they have looking at screens, so staying busy keeps them from having too much screen time.
- Staying busy after school helps kids stay safe, especially if they come home to an empty house.
- After-school activities can be important for getting into college and earning scholarships.

It's not always easy to find your point of view when there are strong feelings on both sides of a debate. Making a chart such as this one can help you **focus** on the most important arguments so you can see which points you agree with.

# GLOSSARY

**anxiety:** A mental condition marked by strong feelings of fear or nervousness about what might happen.

**COVID-19 pandemic:** An event that began in China in 2019 in which a disease that causes breathing problems, a fever, and other health issues spread rapidly around the world and made millions of people sick in a short period of time.

**debate:** An argument or discussion about an issue, generally between two sides.

**expert:** Someone who has a special skill or knowledge.

**focus:** To direct attention or effort at something.

**mental:** Relating to the mind.

**reality:** The way things actually are.

**shelter:** A place that offers food and housing for animals without a home.

**social media:** A collection of websites and applications, or apps, that allow users to interact with each other and create online communities.

**stressed:** Affected by a state of strong feelings of worry.

**tutor:** A private teacher.

**volunteer:** To do something to help because you want to do it.

# For More INFORMATION

## WEBSITES

**KidsHealth: Stress and Coping**
*kidshealth.org/en/kids/center/relax-center.html*
This part of the KidsHealth website offers tips for dealing with stress and anxiety.

**Screen Time vs. Lean Time**
*www.cdc.gov/nccdphp/dnpao/multimedia/infographics/getmoving.html*
Visitors to this U.S. government website can click on an age group to see how much time people in that group spend in front of screens and to get ideas for other ways they can spend their free time.

## BOOKS

Audra, Janari. *Mental Health in Our World*. Buffalo, NY: PowerKids Press, 2022.

Rose, Emily. *Recognizing and Managing Stress*. Ann Arbor, MI: Cherry Lake Publishing, 2022.

Rustad, Martha E. H. *Limit Screen Time*. North Mankato, MN: Pebble, 2020.

# INDEX